Y0-DLF-433

A22100 243916

J 359.325 STE
Stephen, Richard
The picture world of
Aircraft Carriers

DO NOT REMOVE CARD FROM POCKET

10¢ CHARGE FOR EACH LOST
OR DAMAGED CARD.

DUNLAP PUBLIC LIBRARY DISTRICT
DUNLAP, ILLINOIS

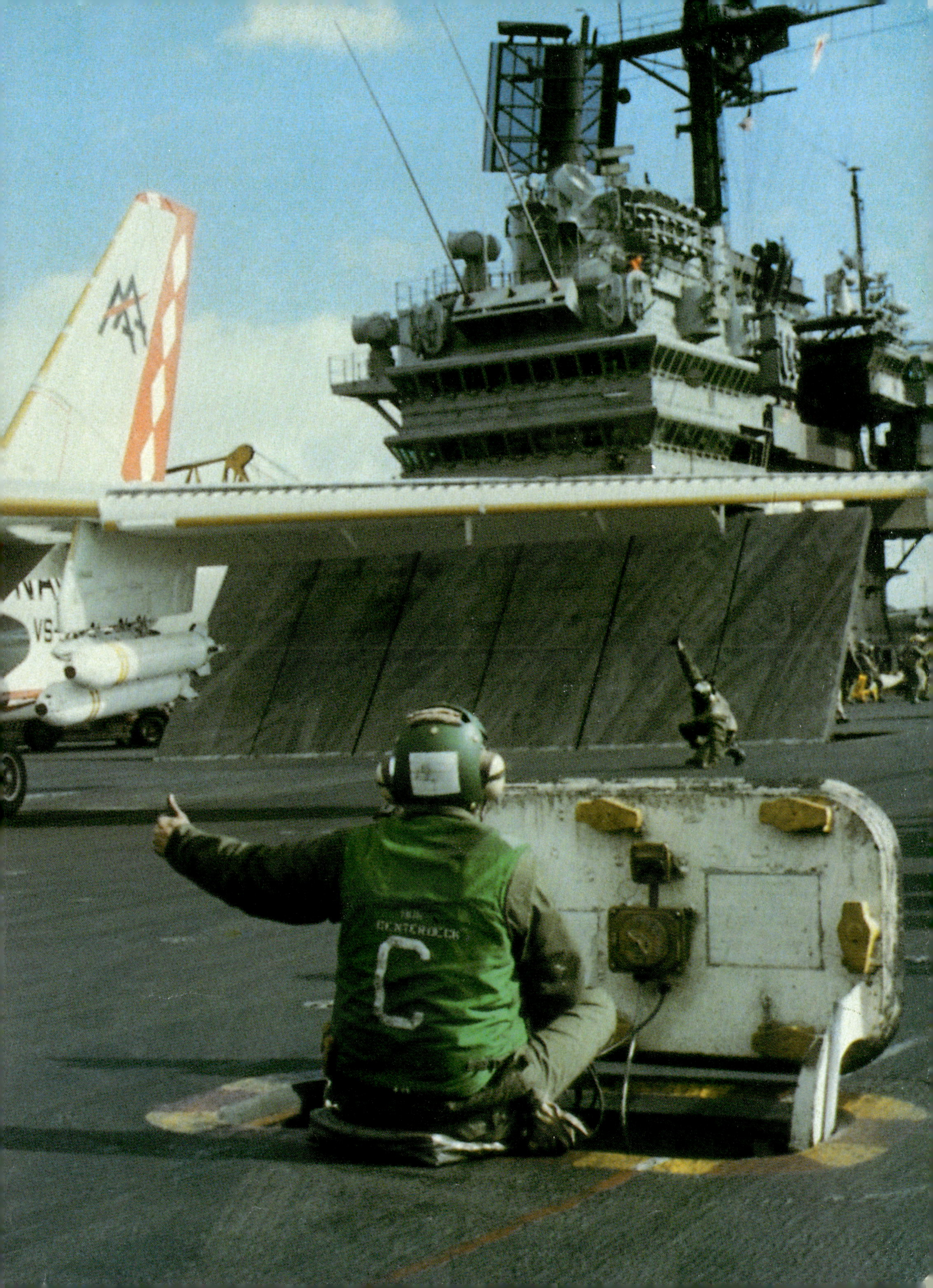
C

© 1990 Franklin Watts

First published in the United
States by
Franklin Watts Inc
387 Park Avenue South
New York
N.Y. 10016

Library of Congress Cataloguing-in-Publication Data
Stephen, R. J.
    Aircraft carriers, R. J. Stephen.
      p. cm. — (Picture world)
    Includes index.
    Summary: Discusses "floating airfields" and their role in maritime air power; how carriers are used in different navies; and the cost and the pros and cons of these enormous ships.
    ISBN 0-531-14008-3
    1. Aircraft carriers—Juvenile literature.   2. Aircraft carriers—
—United States—Juvenile literature.   [1. Aircraft carriers]
I. Title.   II. Series.
V874.B37   1990   89-36500
359.3'25—dc20   CIP
                                                    AC

Printed in Belgium
All rights reserved

Series Editor
Norman Barrett

Designed by
K and Co

Photographs by
British Aerospace
Fleet Photographic (Crown
   Copyright)
U.S. Department of Defense
U.S. Navy

Technical Consultant
Bernie Fitzsimons

The Picture World of

Aircraft Carriers

R. J. Stephen

CONTENTS

Introduction	6
The battle group	8
On deck	9
Below deck	17
Kinds of carriers	18
Facts	26
Glossary	28
Index	29

Franklin Watts
New York • London • Sydney • Toronto

Introduction

An aircraft carrier is a warship with a wide, flat deck used as a runway for aircraft. Modern American carriers are the largest warships afloat. Some carry more than 90 aircraft and 6,000 men.

Some other naval powers have smaller aircraft carriers. These carry helicopters and jump jets, which need very little deck space for taking off and landing.

△ A large, nuclear-powered aircraft carrier with fighters and attack planes parked on deck.

△ A fighter takes off from the front of an aircraft carrier.

▽ Jump jets and helicopters are used with small carriers.

7

The battle group

The large American nuclear-powered carriers are capable of taking massive air power to all parts of the world. Some of this great air power is used for defense against enemy aircraft and submarines.

The carrier operates as part of a battle group, or task force. It is escorted by cruisers, destroyers and submarines. These vessels also help to protect the carrier.

△ An aerial shot of part of a battle group. The nuclear-powered "super-carrier," in the middle, is surrounded by smaller ships of the group. A carrier battle group is more powerful than many of the world's air forces.

On deck

Most of the large carrier deck is used as an airfield. There are airstrips for taking off and landing, and various devices to get the planes into the air and help them to stop when they come down.

The ship is commanded and steered from the island, the structure that rises above the flight deck. This also houses radar and communications equipment.

▽ Some aircraft are stored on deck, while others are brought up from hangars below deck. The island is always on the starboard side – that is, on the right-hand side of the ship looking forward. The ship is controlled from there, as are all movements of aircraft.

All movements on the flight deck are controlled from the Flying Control Position, high up on the island superstructure. The aim is to put the planes into the air safely and as quickly as possible.

The crew on the flight deck wear jackets colored according to the job they do. The men who handle the aircraft weapons, for example, wear red jackets.

△ A plane-handler (in yellow) gives instructions while other crewmen prepare a Tomcat fighter for take off. The green-jackets look after the maintenance of the aircraft, white is for safety and red for the crew who handle the plane's weapons.

△ Steam rises from a launch catapult as a Tomcat fighter moves into position for take-off. The aircraft is hooked onto runners that are shot forward by steam power along tracks in the deck.

▷ Crewmen erect a net on the deck of a carrier. This is a safety device sometimes used to catch any aircraft whose hook misses the wires used to stop them.

▷ Trick photography shows the path of a plane as it catapults off the flight deck at night. The blast shield protects another plane moving up for take off.

△ A blast shield (left) comes up to protect crewmen from the heat and blast of a plane's engines as it prepares to take off.

▷ An aircraft comes to a halt, having hooked on to an arrester wire. These wires, or cables, are stretched out across the deck and the pilot lowers a hook as he lands.

13

Modern aircraft carriers have a landing deck set at an angle to the rest of the flight deck. A pilot who misses the arrester wires can fly off and come back for another landing.

▽ The landing deck, to the right of the picture, is set at an angle to the rest of the flight deck.

▷ Swabbing the deck of a carrier might be a tedious chore, but it's an important one.

▽ The wings of many aircraft that operate from carriers fold in order to take up less space when stored.

15

The smaller carriers are similar in design to their larger cousins. The island is situated on the starboard side, but the flight deck is much smaller, with a steep ramp at the forward end.

△ A jump jet takes to the air from a short ramp. On its return, with less fuel and perhaps minus some missiles, it is lighter and can land vertically.

Below deck

Below the flight deck of a large carrier is the hangar deck. Most of the aircraft are kept there and serviced and repaired in workshops. There are storage areas for spare parts and elevators for moving the aircraft between the flight and hangar decks.

Further down are the crew's living quarters and storage for food, ammunition and fuel.

▽ An aircraft stands on the hangar deck ready to be raised onto the flight deck.

Kinds of carriers

Aircraft carriers may be grouped by class. A class consists of similar ships, and its name is that of the first ship built in that class. The Nimitz class, for example, takes its name from USS *Chester W. Nimitz*.

The Nimitz class also includes the *Dwight D. Eisenhower*, *Carl Vinson* and *Theodore Roosevelt*. These nuclear-powered carriers are the largest ships afloat.

△ Two nuclear-powered carriers take part in an operation in the Indian Ocean, the *Eisenhower* at the front of the picture and the *Nimitz* behind. Compare their size with that of the guided-missile cruiser to the left.

▷ An aerial shot of USS *Carl Vinson*, with more than half its aircraft on deck.

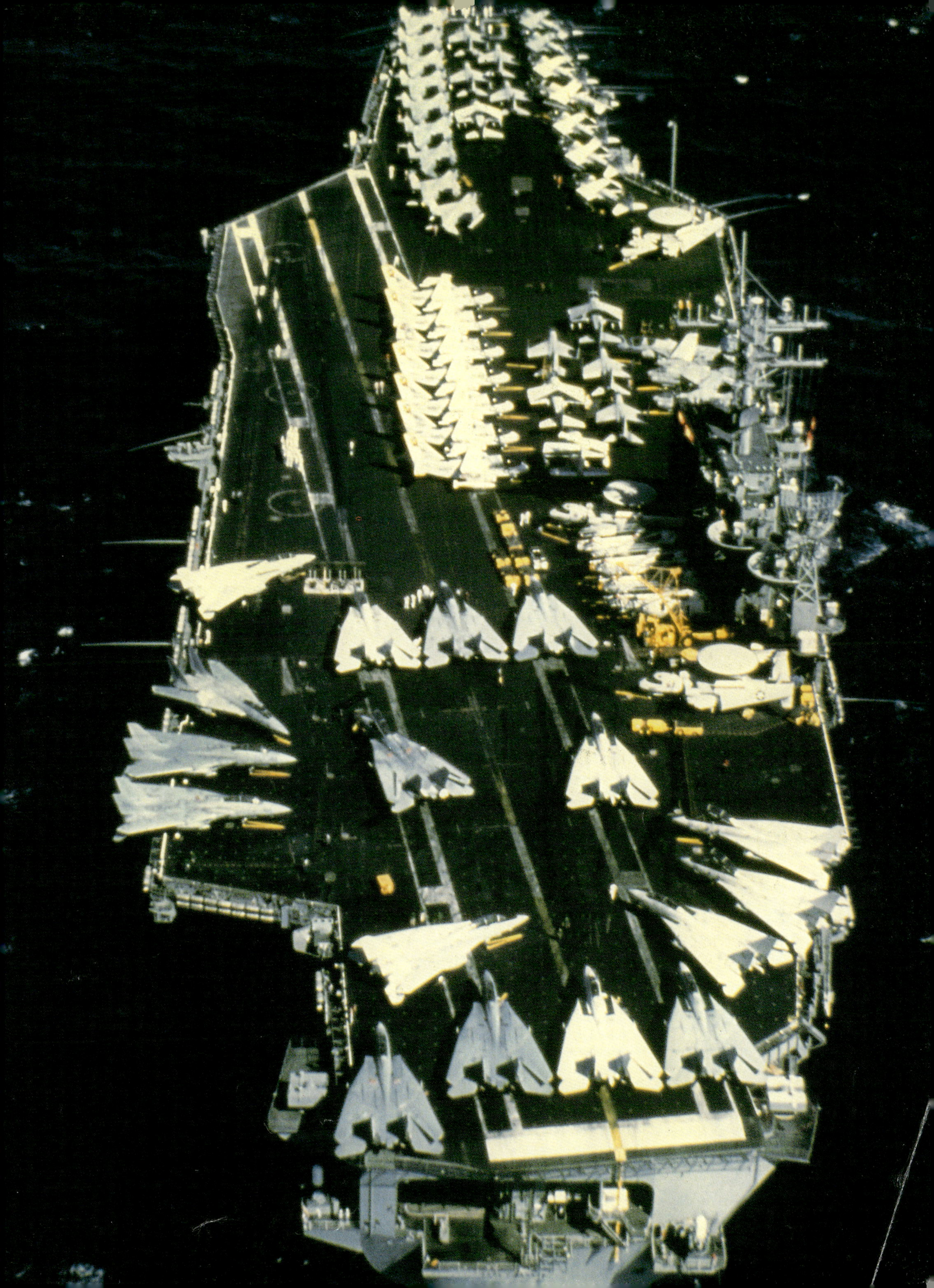

The only other class of nuclear-powered carriers consists of a single ship, the USS *Enterprise*.

The other classes of carriers are oil-powered. The U.S. Navy operates the largest carriers, but other countries such as France and the Soviet Union are building similar vessels. Some navies have anti-submarine and assault carriers.

△ USS *Enterprise* in San Francisco Bay. A ceremony takes place on deck in front of the island, where the ship's name and number are clearly displayed. Nuclear-powered carriers are denoted by the letters CVN, and the *Enterprise* is No. 65.

▷ USS *America* of the Kitty Hawk class.

21

▷ Sailors man the rails of the *John F. Kennedy* as it enters Boston harbor. The carrier is slightly larger than her sister ships of the Kitty Hawk class, and is officially listed as the only ship of a separate class.

◁ The USS *Forrestal* in the Suez Canal, with a formation of crewmen spelling out "108," the number of days the ship had been at sea. The four Forrestal class ships, built in the 1950s, were the first carriers to handle jet aircraft. They were overhauled in the 1980s.

△ The crew man the rails of the *Coral Sea* as a tug nudges her into port. The *Coral Sea* and her sister ship the *Midway* are the only American carriers from World War II still in service.

▷ The *Tarawa* can carry up to 30 helicopters. Officially classed as amphibious assault ships, Tarawa class carriers measure about three-quarters the length of an attack carrier.

Assault carriers, or amphibious assault ships, land marines by helicopter. They also have landing craft for putting men and equipment on shore.

Anti-submarine carriers use helicopters to search for and destroy submarines. They have jump jets for air defense.

△ HMS *Ark Royal* in Hong Kong harbor. The British Navy has three of these Invincible class anti-submarine carriers.

▷ The *Minsk*, a carrier of the Kiev class. These Soviet anti-submarine ships are the world's most heavily armed carriers.

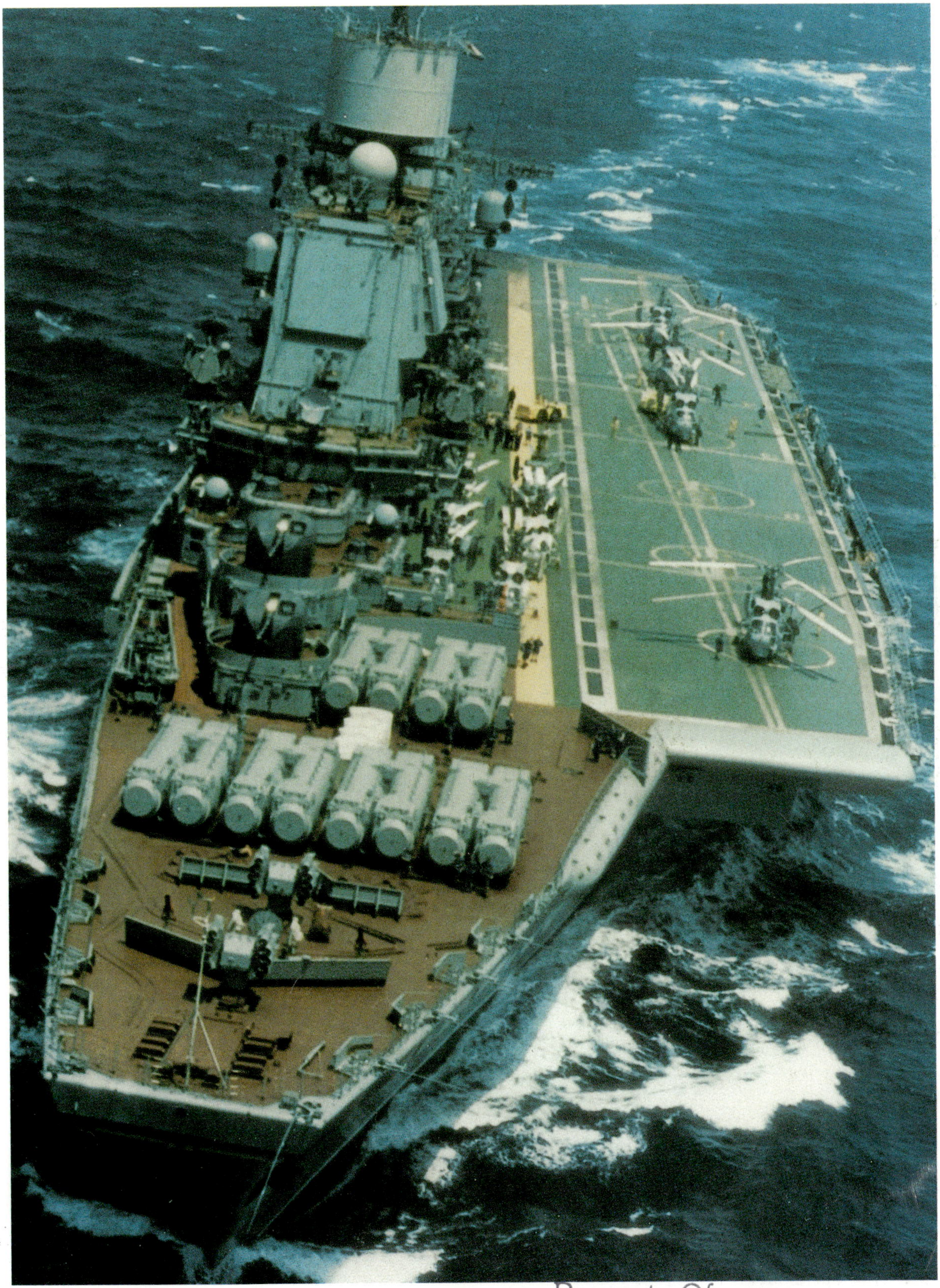

Facts

Nuclear fuel
Each Nimitz class carrier is powered by two nuclear reactors with enough fuel to steam a million miles (1.6 million km).

Speed
The big attack carriers are all capable of speeds greater than 30 knots (55.5 km/h or 34.5 mph).

△ The *Carl Vinson*, a Nimitz class carrier, is powered by nuclear fuel.

Attack carriers
The United States Navy entered the 1990s with 15 large attack carriers capable of operating with conventional aircraft. They are sometimes called CTOL carriers, for Conventional Take Off and Landing. Of these, five were nuclear-powered, with another two Nimitz class carriers in production.

The only other nations with plans for building attack carriers are France and the Soviet Union.

Longest
The nuclear-powered carrier USS *Enterprise* is the longest warship in the world, with an overall length of 1,102 ft (335.9 meters). It is just 10 ft (3 m) longer than the Nimitz class carriers. But the Nimitz carriers are heavier.

△ The *Enterprise*, the longest warship afloat.

26

A lesson learned

In the last years of World War II, a desperate Japanese Air Force used "kamikaze" pilots to crash their planes onto Allied ships, sinking some and damaging many others. Although no aircraft carriers were sunk by these suicide missions, the wooden flight decks of some American carriers were severely damaged, whereas the attackers bounced off the metal decks of British carriers.

As a result, the U.S. Navy began to build carriers with flight decks made of solid steel, 3 1/2 in (9 cm) thick. The first of these carriers, the *Midway*, came into active service just after the end of the war, in September 1945, and together with her sister ship the *Coral Sea*, is still in service today.

△ The *Midway*, still in service after more than 40 years.

Crew

Nimitz class carriers go to sea with about 6,300 men. Of these, 3,300 are the ship's crew and officers, while 3,000 are assigned to the air wing.

FOD

Jet engines suck in air with tremendous force when an aircraft is about to take off. Damage sometimes occurs to the fan blades of an engine if an object is sucked into it. This is called Foreign Object Damage or FOD.

△ The crew muster on deck of the *Kitty Hawk* to celebrate 100 days of flight operations without any FOD (foreign object damage).

27

Glossary

Air wing
The crew and officers on a carrier concerned with the aircraft, from pilots to workshop maintenance mechanics.

Amphibious assault ship
A small carrier used to land troops and equipment on shore.

Arrester wires
Cables stretched across the landing deck to help stop the aircraft. A pilot lowers a hook from the back of the plane as he touches down and the hook catches on one of the arrester wires.

Battle group
A force of ships, usually centered on an aircraft carrier and helping to protect it while the group carries out its mission; also called a task force.

Blast shield
A barrier that is raised behind a plane that is about to take off to protect crew and other aircraft from the blast of its engines.

Catapult
A device used to give an aircraft enough deck speed for a safe launch.

Conventional aircraft
A plane that takes off and lands in the regular way, with a high deck speed.

Flight deck
The main deck of an aircraft carrier from which the aircraft take off.

Island
The structure, also called the superstructure, that rises from the deck of a carrier and houses various control rooms. It is always located to starboard — the right-hand side, looking forward.

Superstructure
See *Island*.

Task force
Same as *Battle group*.

Index

air wing 27, 28
America 21
amphibious assault ship 23, 24, 28
Ark Royal 24
arrester wire 12, 14, 28
assault carrier 20, 24
attack carrier 6, 23, 26

battle group 8, 28
blast shield 12, 13, 28

Carl Vinson 18
catapult 11, 28
class 18
conventional aircraft 26, 28
Coral Sea 23, 27
crew 27
CTOL carrier 26

deck, angled 14

Eisenhower 18
Enterprise 20, 26

fighter 6, 7, 10
flight deck 9, 10, 12, 14, 16, 17, 27, 28
flying control position 10
foreign object damage 27
Forrestal 22
Forrestal class 22
fuel 17, 27

hangar 9, 17
helicopter 6, 7, 23, 24

Invincible class 24

island 9, 10, 16, 20, 28

jump jet 6, 16, 24

Kennedy 22
Kiev class 25
Kitty Hawk class 21, 22

landing craft 24
living quarters 17

marines 24
Midway 23, 27
Minsk 25

Nimitz 18
Nimitz class 18, 26, 27
nuclear-powered carrier 6, 8, 18, 20, 26
nuclear reactor 27

radar 9
ramp 16

safety 10, 11
speed 26
starboard 9, 16
submarine 8, 24
superstructure 10, 28

take off 11, 13
Tarawa 23
Tarawa class 23
task force 8, 28

wings, folding 15
World War II 23, 27

29

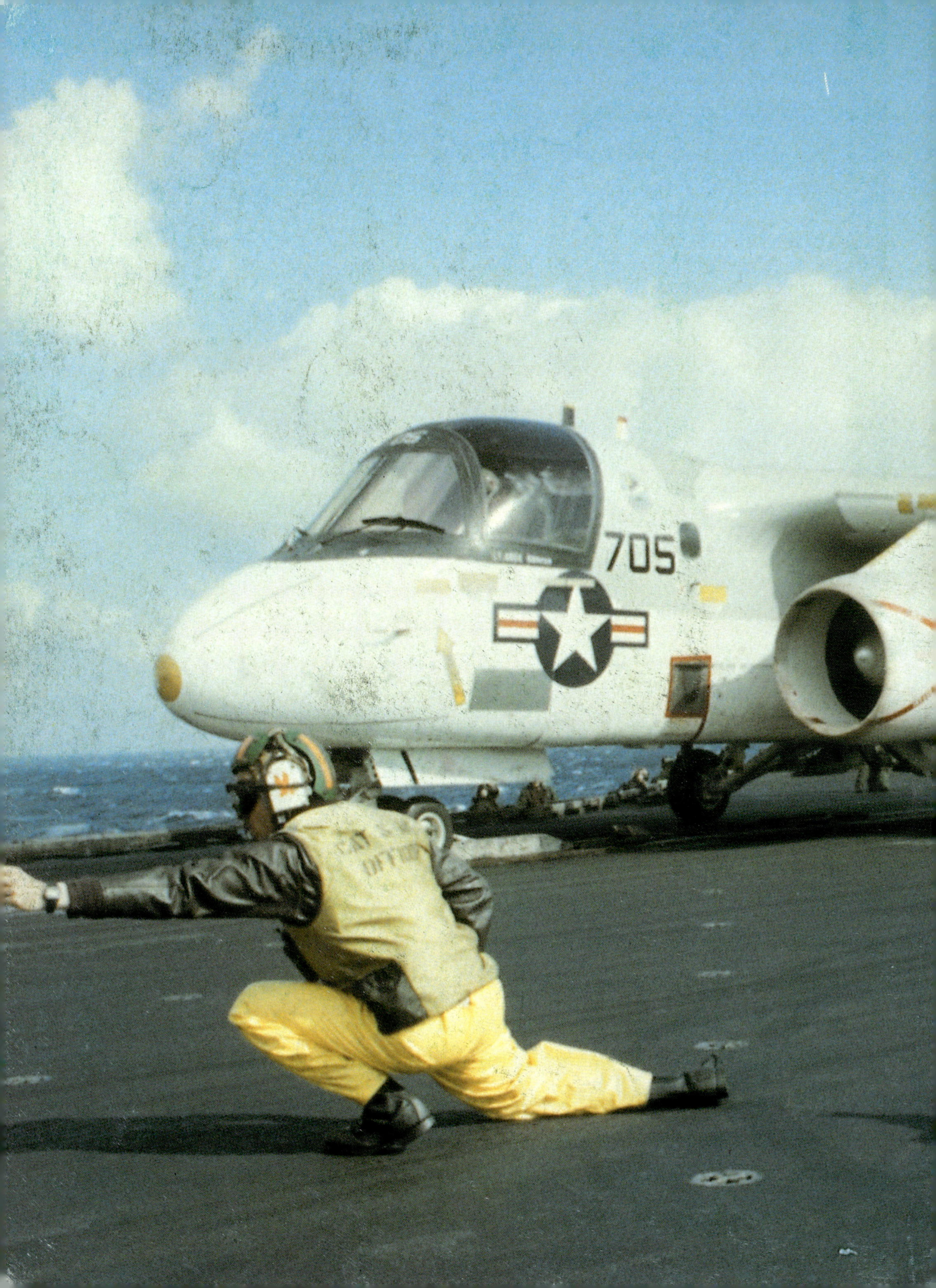
705